Animal Adaptations

Migration

Megan Kopp

MEDIA ENHANCED BOOKS

AV2 BY WEIGL

ADDED VALUE • AUDIO VISUAL

www.av2books.com

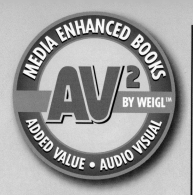

AV² provides enriched content that supplements and complements this book. Weigl's AV² books strive to create inspired learning and engage young minds in a total learning experience.

Your AV² Media Enhanced books come alive with...

Audio
Listen to sections of the book read aloud.

Key Words
Study vocabulary, and complete a matching word activity.

Video
Watch informative video clips.

Quizzes
Test your knowledge.

Go to **www.av2books.com**, and enter this book's unique code.

BOOK CODE

W 9 7 6 9 5 7

Embedded Weblinks
Gain additional information for research.

Slide Show
View images and captions, and prepare a presentation.

AV² by Weigl brings you media enhanced books that support active learning.

Try This!
Complete activities and hands-on experiments.

... and much, much more!

Published by AV² by Weigl
350 5th Avenue, 59th Floor
New York, NY 10118
Website: www.av2books.com

Library of Congress Cataloging-in-Publication Data
Kopp, Megan.
Migration / Megan Kopp.
  pages cm. -- (Animal adaptations)
Includes bibliographical references and index.
ISBN 978-1-4896-3679-9 (hard cover : alk. paper) -- ISBN 978-1-4896-3680-5 (soft cover : alk. paper) -- ISBN 978-1-4896-3681-2 (single user ebook) -- ISBN 978-1-4896-3682-9 (multi-user ebook)
1. Animal migration--Juvenile literature. I. Title.
QL754.K665 2015
591.56'8--dc23

                    2015000821

Printed in the United States of America in Brainerd, Minnesota
1 2 3 4 5 6 7 8 9 19 18 17 16 15

052015
WEP051515

Project Coordinator Aaron Carr
Art Director Terry Paulhus

Every reasonable effort has been made to trace ownership and to obtain permission to reprint copyright material. The publishers would be pleased to have any errors or omissions brought to their attention so that they may be corrected in subsequent printings.

Photo Credits
Weigl acknowledges Getty Images as its primary photo supplier for this title.

Contents

What Is an Adaptation?

Animals have different characteristics, or traits, that allow them to survive in their **habitat**. It can take millions of years for these traits to develop. Over time, the traits best suited to an environment are passed on through **natural selection**. The animals that have adapted best to their habitat are able to survive for many **generations**.

There are many different types of adaptations. Adaptations are useful for finding food, finding a **mate**, movement, and surviving in a changing habitat. Some animals have developed special skills that allow them to travel, or migrate, long distances from one habitat to another. Many types of birds have adapted to migrate as the seasons change.

Wildebeests live in Africa. Each year they travel more than 1,000 miles (1,600 kilometers) in search of food, crossing lakes and rivers as they go.

5

AMAZING ADAPTATIONS

Many animals use the Sun and stars to find their way when they migrate. Some use Earth's **magnetic field** or a special light.

European Starling

Starlings migrate to warmer places for the winter. They find their way by using the movement of the Sun across the sky.

Swainson's Thrush

Songbirds that migrate at night, such as the Swainson's thrush, often use the movement of groups of stars to find their way.

Sockeye Salmon

Earth's magnetic field helps to guide salmon back to their home rivers.

Tiger Salamander

Salamanders can use a special light pattern to tell where the Sun is, even on cloudy days.

Gray Whale

Scientists think that whales use features of the coastline to find their way as they migrate.

What Is Migration?

Migration is a regular move from one place to another. It is usually seasonal. The move to a different place is always followed by a journey to the starting place. From bats to butterflies, many animal **species** migrate. A migration can cover a short or long distance. It can go from north to south, east to west, or up and down a mountain. **Plankton** migrate vertically every day. They move up and down in water. Migration is movement in one direction and back again for a reason.

Monarch butterflies in North America migrate in fall to spend winter in a warmer climate. They return in spring.

OVER LAND

Toads, lemmings, and snakes are among the many species that migrate over land. Large African animals, such as elephants and zebras, migrate for food and water. Herds of caribou migrate south to avoid the harsh winters of the open **tundra**.

IN WATER

Many **aquatic** species migrate, including penguins, whales, and eels. Northern fur seals travel to southwestern Alaska every summer to reproduce. Antarctic whales migrate long distances every year to warmer waters.

BY AIR

Warblers, some dragonflies, and Mexican free-tailed bats are among the species that migrate by air. Most birds that migrate usually travel at a low **altitude**. They fly just a few hundred feet (meters) above the ground. Migrating bar-headed geese, however, have been recorded flying at 29,500 feet (9,000 m).

How Do Animals Use Migration?

Some animals avoid cold weather and food shortages by **hibernating**. Some animals adapt to their environment and stay active year-round. Other animals migrate.

Migration helps these animals survive. When food becomes scarce in one area, or the weather becomes too cold, these animals move to another place. Often, this migration is seasonal, based on what food is available at a particular time of the year. In Africa, wildebeests follow the rain. A **cyclical** pattern of rainfall provides moisture for grass to grow. The grass feeds the herds.

Migration is risky. For most animals, migration takes a lot of energy and time. Animals that migrate are active and more likely to be seen by **predators**. They must deal with bad weather. There is a chance that they will not have enough food or energy to be able to complete their journey.

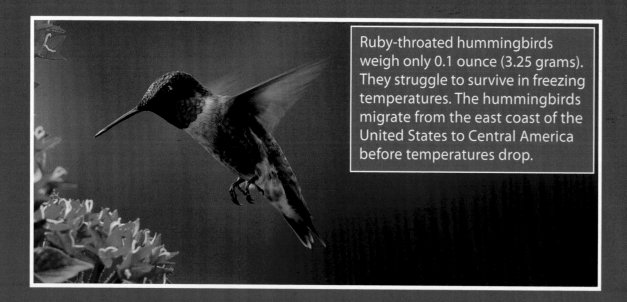

Ruby-throated hummingbirds weigh only 0.1 ounce (3.25 grams). They struggle to survive in freezing temperatures. The hummingbirds migrate from the east coast of the United States to Central America before temperatures drop.

African Savanna Food Chain

In a food chain, producers are plants such as grass and bushes. Producers gather energy from the Sun. Wildebeests are primary consumers. These **herbivores** eat the grass that grows on the **savanna**. Secondary consumers are large animals that eat other animals for food. Crocodiles catch the migrating wildebeests as they cross rivers. Lions catch weak wildebeests that drop back from the herd. Decomposers complete the cycle. Dung beetles are decomposers that break down the waste of plant-eating animals.

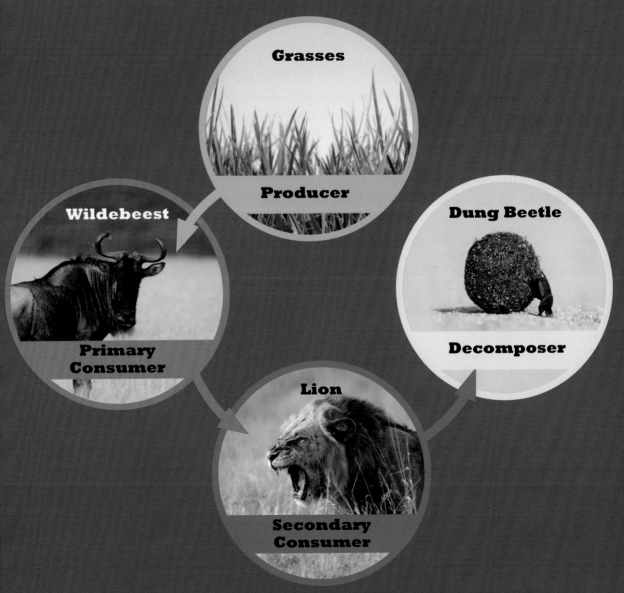

Grasses — Producer

Wildebeest — Primary Consumer

Lion — Secondary Consumer

Dung Beetle — Decomposer

Types of Migration

There are many types of migration. In North America, birds that migrate travel along one of three different north-to-south routes, called flyways. The Atlantic and Pacific Flyways follow the east and west coastlines. The Central Flyway follows the spine of the Rocky Mountains.

Caribou migrate hundreds of miles (km) from winter to summer ranges and back again. The path they follow is not always the same. Elk migrate up and down mountains. After the first heavy storm in fall, spiny lobsters walk in single file from shallow to deep water. They travel about 20 miles (32 km) to where the water is calmer.

In spring, elk migrate up mountains to graze. In winter, they move to lower slopes to graze on the grass under the snow.

5

SUPER MIGRATORS

Longest Insect Migration

Monarch butterflies travel up to 2,950 miles (4,750 km), from North America to their wintering grounds in Mexico. They save energy by using the wind to carry them.

Champion Fliers

Arctic terns fly about 22,000 miles (35,000 km) from their Arctic breeding grounds to Antarctica and back. This is equal to flying to the moon and back three times.

Largest Land Mammal Migration

More than 1.5 million wildebeests migrate in a gigantic loop every year. They follow the rains and green grasses. About 250,000 of them die during the journey.

Longest Ocean Migration

Leatherback turtles migrate farther than any other kind of sea turtle. One leatherback turtle was recorded traveling 12,774 miles (20,558 km) in less than two years.

Longest Mammal Migration in Water

Humpback whales travel up to 5,280 miles (8,500 km) each way between their summer feeding grounds near the North and South Poles and their winter breeding grounds near the equator.

How Does It Work?

Migration takes animals to areas where their needs can be met. For some birds, this can involve long flights at a high altitude. As a result, migratory birds have special adaptations to help them make the journey.

Migrating birds usually have longer and more pointed wings than birds that do not migrate. This helps reduce air **resistance** and saves energy. Migrating birds have larger chest muscles and hearts than other birds. They begin feeding heavily several weeks before their migratory flights. This is called **hyperphagia**. The longer the flight, the more fat the birds need to store.

Bar-tailed godwits go south for the winter, all the way from Alaska to New Zealand. The birds have been known to fly 7,000 miles (11,000 km) without eating, drinking, or resting.

FOUR WAYS TO PREPARE FOR MIGRATION

Weight Gain

Insects and birds gain weight before migration. Ruby-throated hummingbirds can often double their weight. This stored fat gives them energy.

New Feathers

Most birds in North America grow new feathers before the fall migration. This helps increase flight speed and efficiency.

Safety in Numbers

Traveling in a flock increases safety for migrating birds and helps them **navigate** and find food. Canada geese form a V-shape when they migrate. This makes flying less tiring. As the lead bird tires, it falls back and another takes its place at the front.

Early Birds to Night Owls

Most songbirds are active during daylight hours. When they migrate, they fly at night because it is safer. They feed during the day. It is also cooler at night, so the birds do not overheat. Blackpoll warblers migrate up to 2,500 miles (4,000 km).

Timeline

The Earth has warmed and cooled over time. Migration patterns have changed as well. Open tundra slowly moved northward after the end of the last ice age, a period when much of Earth was covered in ice. Species such as caribou and tundra swans now have a slightly longer migration route than they did 10,000 years ago.

The need to migrate has developed slowly over time. Earth's climate changed very quickly after the last ice age. This affected many animals' habitats. The animals that did not move to find food or escape extreme temperatures did not survive. The animals that migrated did survive.

Not all animal species migrate. Animal species that live in tropical forests have warmth and food all year long. They do not need to move.

Salmon spend most of their lives in the ocean but undertake a long migration to breed in the same fresh water where they hatched.

Tracking Migration

20,000 years ago

Stone Age rock art shows animals migrating.

350 BC

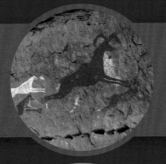

Greek scientist Aristotle notes that some birds come and go in a regular pattern. He believes that summer birds change into different species in the winter.

AD 1899

Hans Christian Mortensen, a Danish scientist known for studying birds, invented a technique called banding. Putting numbered leg bands with contact information on birds helped track their location.

1950s

Radio transmitters are first used by researchers to track wildlife.

2016

The International Cooperation for Animal Research Using Space (ICARUS) system is set to be installed on the International Space Station. It will enable the migratory behavior of very small animals to be studied from space.

How Humans Use Migration

When the word "migration" is used about humans, it usually refers to people leaving a place permanently. One of the greatest human migrations was when people followed the land bridge across the Bering Strait during the last ice age. As the climate warmed, glaciers melted and sea levels rose. This blocked a return migration.

Humans who move with the seasons are called nomads. In prehistoric times, hunter-gatherers migrated to follow food sources. Some people, such as the San people of the Kalahari in Africa, still live this way. Others, including many people in Mongolia, move with the seasons to find food for their **livestock**. People who live this way are called pastoralists.

Kazakh nomads live in Mongolia. Today, they continue to live a semi-nomadic lifestyle.

Humans have learned from the adaptations that animals have made for migration. Fighter pilots sometimes fly in the same V formation as Canada geese. This helps communication and cooperation within their group. Loggerhead turtle hatchlings navigate using the Earth's magnetic field. People use compasses to find their way. Compass needles point to the top of the Earth's magnetic field.

Birds save energy by flying in a V formation. Pilots copy this practice to save fuel.

Migration and Biodiversity

Biodiversity refers to the variety of plants, animals, and other living things in an area. The survival of many living things depends on maintaining biodiversity. Biodiversity helps to keep an environment healthy. An environment with biodiversity is more likely to have enough food for all of the animals in it.

Many people are working to protect sea turtle hatchlings by incubating the eggs away from predators. Then, they release the hatchlings on dark, quiet beaches.

Loss of biodiversity can cause species to become extinct. In turn, loss of species affects biodiversity. Migration aids biodiversity by helping species survive. It is not just good for the species that migrate, but also for all the species within their environment. Many migratory species are **pollinators**. During migration, they spread pollen to distant places. Birds maintain plant biodiversity by spreading seeds in their droppings as they migrate. Some birds help control insect populations as they pass through an area.

Wildlife crossings over or under highways are a way of protecting migrating animals from the dangers of traffic.

Conservation

Migratory animals rely on many different habitats. In the summer, they need breeding areas. Many migrating animals need stopover areas along their journey. In the winter, migrants need feeding and resting areas. In some places, human activity interferes with migration. Open spaces and migratory pathways are being lost to housing, roads, wind farms, and mining. Lights and development along coastlines can interfere with sea turtles' navigation.

The loss of habitat is one of the main threats to migratory birds. The International Union for Conservation of Nature is a worldwide organization helping to protect animals and their habitats. It works to conserve biodiversity around the world.

As cities grow, houses are built on open land. Often, this means that migrating animals lose their resting places.

Activity

Match each animal with one way it adapts for migration.

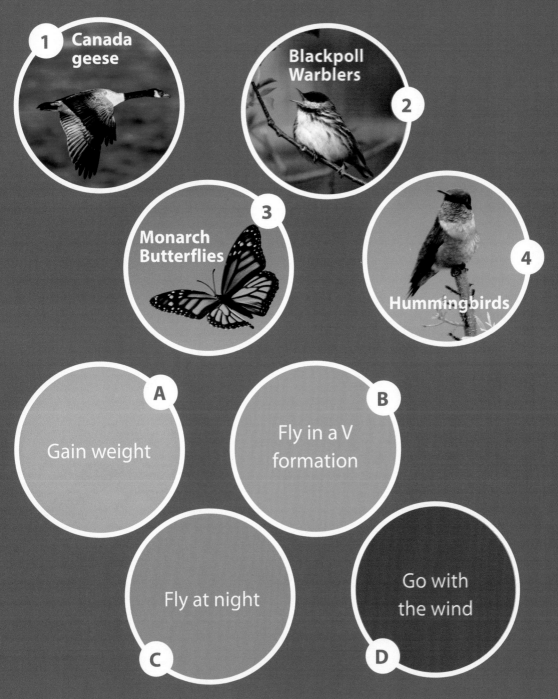

1 Canada geese

2 Blackpoll Warblers

3 Monarch Butterflies

4 Hummingbirds

A Gain weight

B Fly in a V formation

C Fly at night

D Go with the wind

Answers: 1. B 2. C 3. D 4. A

Quiz

Complete this quiz to test your knowledge of migration.

1 Which animal uses a pattern of light to find their way?

A. Tiger salamander

2 Which animal uses features of the coastline to navigate?

A. Gray whale

3 How far do Arctic terns migrate?

A. 22,000 miles (35,000 km)

4 When were radio transmitters first used to track wildlife?

A. In the 1950s

5 What is the highest recorded migration flight?

A. 29,500 feet (9,000 m)

6 Canada Geese migrate in what kind of formation?

A. V formation

7 How many wildebeests migrate each year?

A. More than 1.5 million

8 What are three reasons for animal migration?

A. To find food, escape extreme heat or cold, and reproduce

9 Who was the first person to tag birds with numbers?

A. Hans Christian Mortensen

10 What is over-eating in migrating animals called?

A. Hyperphagia

Key Words

altitude: the height of something above the ground

aquatic: describing an animal that lives in the water

cyclical: happening over and over again in the same order

generations: relating to the normal life span of an animal

habitat: the natural environment of a living thing

herbivores: animals that feed on plants

hibernating: sleeping for the entire winter

hyperphagia: an increased appetite that leads to over-eating

livestock: animals that are kept and raised by humans

magnetic field: a field of magnetism created by Earth's metal core that protects Earth from the Sun's harmful rays

mate: a breeding partner

natural selection: a process whereby animals that are better adapted to their environment survive and pass on those adaptations to their young

navigate: to find the way

plankton: tiny animals or plants that drift or float in oceans or lakes

pollinators: birds or insects that pollinate flowers

predators: animals that hunt and eat other animals

resistance: the force of air that pushes against a bird and slows it down as it flies

savanna: a large, flat area of land covered in grass, with only a few trees or bushes

species: a group of plants or animals that are alike in many ways

tundra: a cold area in the north where there are no trees and the ground under the surface is always frozen

Index

Log on to www.av2books.com

AV² by Weigl brings you media enhanced books that support active learning. Go to www.av2books.com, and enter the special code found on page 2 of this book. You will gain access to enriched and enhanced content that supplements and complements this book. Content includes video, audio, weblinks, quizzes, a slide show, and activities.

AV² Online Navigation

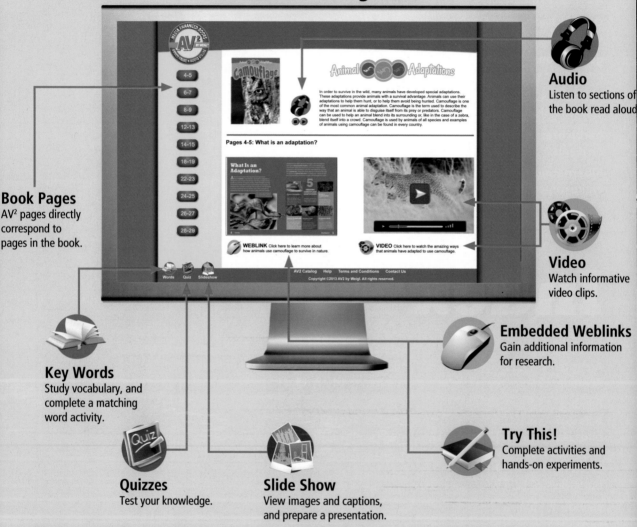

Audio
Listen to sections of the book read aloud

Book Pages
AV² pages directly correspond to pages in the book.

Video
Watch informative video clips.

Key Words
Study vocabulary, and complete a matching word activity.

Embedded Weblinks
Gain additional information for research.

Quizzes
Test your knowledge.

Slide Show
View images and captions, and prepare a presentation.

Try This!
Complete activities and hands-on experiments.

AV² was built to bridge the gap between print and digital. We encourage you to tell us what you like and what you want to see in the future.

Sign up to be an AV² Ambassador at www.av2books.com/ambassador.